Ex Libris

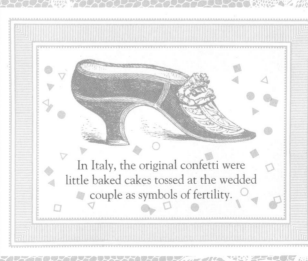

In Italy, the original confetti were little baked cakes tossed at the wedded couple as symbols of fertility.

Stop!

Slip this card out of this
pocket page.
Your Snapshot
Keepsake Book
instructions
are on the back sid

Copyright © 1991 by
Marquand Books, Inc. and Michele Durkson Clise
A Snap Book*
All rights reserved. No part of this book may be reproduced in any form
without written permission from the publisher.
Produced and designed by Marquand Books, Inc.
Printed in Hong Kong
ISBN: 0-8118-9035-x

"As I Walk Out One Evening" from *W. H. Auden: Collected Poems* by W. H.
Auden, ed. by Edward Mendelson. Copyright 1940 and renewed 1968 by W
H. Auden. Reprinted by permission of Random House, Inc.

Distributed in Canada by Raincoast Books
112 East 3rd Avenue, Vancouver, B.C. V5T1C8
1 3 5 7 9 10 8 6 4 2
Chronicle Books
275 Fifth Street, San Francisco, California 94103

OUR
WEDDING
KEEPSAKE

A SNAPSHOT
KEEPSAKE
BOOK

MICHELE DURKSON CLISE

Chronicle Books
San Francisco

FIRST MEETING

A tender, sensitive young female tells
how she felt when first he kissed her—
like a tub of roses swimming in honey,
cologne, nutmeg, and blackberries.

—S. S. Cox, 1876

THE PROPOSAL

~~~~~~

~~~~~~

~~~~~~

~~~~~~

~~~~~~

~~~~~~

~~~~~~

~~~~~~

Rosy apple, lemon and pear,
Bunch of roses she shall wear,
Gold and silver by her side,
I know who shall be my bride.
—LONDON CHILDREN'S STREET CHANT

NAME

BIRTHDATE

BIRTHPLACE

MOTHER

FATHER

The Bride

_____

NAME

_____

BIRTHDATE

_____

BIRTHPLACE

_____

MOTHER

_____

FATHER

The Groom

THE CEREMONY

Something old, something new, something borrowed,

I'll love you, dear,
I'll love you
Till China and Africa
meet
And the river jumps
over the mountain
And the salmon sing
in the street.

THE CEREMONY

something blue, and a lucky penny in her shoe.

> I'll love you till the ocean
> Is folded and hung up
> to dry
> And the seven stars go
> squawking
> Like geese about the sky.
> —W. H. AUDEN

Seeing an elephant, a black cat, or a chimney-sweep on her way to the church is considered a sign of luck for the bride.

TIME

PLACE

OFFICIAL

WEDDING DETAILS

WEDDING DETAILS

THE WEDDING PARTY

Bridesmaids traditionally dressed in the same clothes as the bride to baffle evil spirits.

~~~~~~~~~~~~~~~~~~~~~~~~~~~~~~~~

~~~~~~~~~~~~~~~~~~~~~~~~~~~~~~~~

~~~~~~~~~~~~~~~~~~~~~~~~~~~~~~~~

~~~~~~~~~~~~~~~~~~~~~~~~~~~~~~~~

~~~~~~~~~~~~~~~~~~~~~~~~~~~~~~~~

~~~~~~~~~~~~~~~~~~~~~~~~~~~~~~~~

~~~~~~~~~~~~~~~~~~~~~~~~~~~~~~~~

~~~~~~~~~~~~~~~~~~~~~~~~~~~~~~~~

THE WEDDING PARTY

According to Greek tradition, a bride will bring sweetness to her marriage by putting a piece of sugar in her glove.

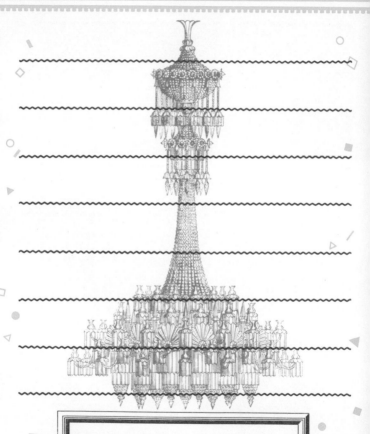

A kiss is worth nothing until it's
divided between two.
—GYPSY PROVERB

WEDDING MEMORIES

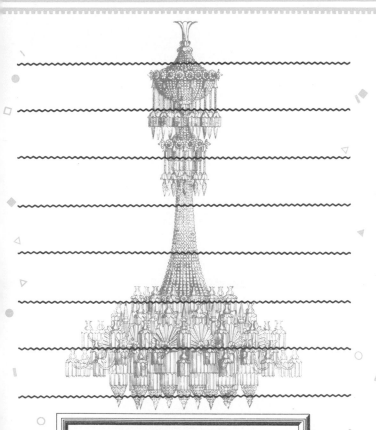

I will make you brooches
and toys for your delight,
Of bird-song at morning
and star-shine at night.
—ROBERT LOUIS STEVENSON

FLORAL TRADITION

Here are fruits, flowers,
leaves and branches, ...
here is my heart.

—VERLAINE

The Bride's Bouquet

FLORAL TRADITION

Come live with me and be my Love
And I will make thee beds of roses
And a thousand fragrant posies.
—CHRISTOPHER MARLOWE

Our Favorite Flowers

~~~~~~

~~~~~~

~~~~~~

Yes, we must ever be friends;
and of all who offer you friendship,
let me ever be the first, the truest,
the nearest, the dearest.
—LONGFELLOW

FAMILY AND FRIENDS

Let all the joys be as the month of May.

FAMILY AND FRIENDS

And all thy days be as a marriage day.

THE GUEST LIST

THE RECEPTION

THE RECEPTION

*They dined on mince, and slices of quince,
Which they ate with a runcible spoon;*

THE WEDDING FEAST

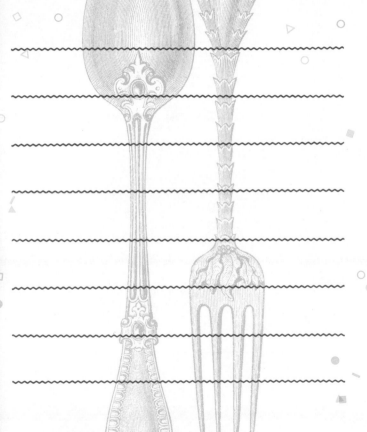

And hand in hand, on the edge of the sand,
They danced by the light of the moon.

—Edward Lear, The Owl and the Pussycat

And as this round
Is nowhere found
To flaw, or else to sever,
So may our love
As endless prove,
As pure as gold for ever.

MUSIC

~~~~~~

~~~~~~

~~~~~~

~~~~~~

~~~~~~

~~~~~~

How silver-sweet sound lovers' tongues by night.

MUSIC

~~~~~~

~~~~~~

~~~~~~

~~~~~~

~~~~~~

~~~~~~

~~~~~~

~~~~~~

Like soft music to attending ears. —William Shakespeare

Who travels for love finds a thousand miles

THE HONEYMOON

not longer than one. — Japanese Proverb

THE HONEYMOON

A HONEYMOON

~~~~~~

~~~~~~

~~~~~~

~~~~~~

~~~~~~

~~~~~~

But of all the lunar things that change,
The one that shows most fickle and strange,

TRAVELOGUE

~~~~~~

~~~~~~

~~~~~~

~~~~~~

~~~~~~

~~~~~~

And takes the most eccentric range,
Is the moon—so called—of honey!
—Thomas Hood

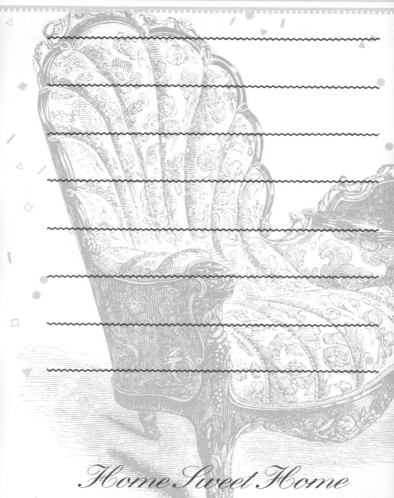

AT HOME AT LAST

~~~~~~

~~~~~~

~~~~~~

~~~~~~

~~~~~~

~~~~~~

~~~~~~

~~~~~~

Home Sweet Home

At Home at Last

Home Sweet Home

Birthstones and Flowers

January
Garnet
Carnation or Snowdrop

§

February
Amethyst
Primrose or Violet

§

March
Aquamarine or
Bloodstone
Jonquil or Daffodil

§

April
Diamond or Rock Crystal
Daisy or Sweet Pea

§

May
Emerald
Hawthorn or
Lily of the Valley

§

June
Moonstone or Pearl
Rose or Honeysuckle

July
Ruby or Cornelian
Water Lily, Larkspur, or
Delphinium

§

August
Peridot or Sardonyx
Gladiolus or Poppy

§

September
Sapphire or Lapis Lazuli
Morning Glory or Aster

§

October
Opal or Tourmaline
Calendula or Marigold

§

November
Topaz
Chrysanthemum

§

December
Turquoise
Holly, Narcissus, or
Poinsetta

BIRTHDAYS

Traditional Gifts

1st Paper
2nd Cotton
3rd Leather
4th Flowers or fruit
5th Wood
6th Sugar or candy
7th Wool
8th Bronze
9th Pottery
10th Tin
11th Steel
12th Linen or silk
13th Lace
14th Agate
15th Crystal
20th China
25th Silver
30th Pearl
35th Coral or jade
40th Ruby or garnet
45th Sapphire or tourmaline
50th Gold
55th Emerald or turquoise
60th Diamond

ANNIVERSARIES

The critical period of matrimony is breakfast time.

— A. P. Herbert